P9-CBK-798

STEM *trailblazer* BIOS

ASTRONAUT
MAE JEMISON

ALLISON LASSIEUR

Lerner Publications • Minneapolis

Lerner Publications Company
A division of Lerner Publishing Group, Inc.
241 First Avenue North
Minneapolis, MN 55401 U.S.A.

For reading levels and more information, look up this title at www.lernerbooks.com.

Content Consultant: Dr. Gregory L. Vogt, Assistant Professor of Allied Health Sciences, Baylor College of Medicine

Library of Congress Cataloging-in-Publication Data

Names: Lassieur, Allison, author.
Title: Astronaut Mae Jemison / by Allison Lassieur.
Description: Minneapolis : Lerner Publications, 2017. | Series: STEM trailblazer bios | Includes
    bibliographical references and index.
Identifiers: LCCN 2015050918 (print) | LCCN 2016000098 (ebook) | ISBN 9781512407914 (lb : alk.
    paper) | ISBN 9781512413113 (pb : alk. paper) | ISBN 9781512410945 (eb pdf)
Subjects: LCSH: Jemison, Mae, 1956—Juvenile literature. | African American women astronauts—
    Biography—Juvenile literature. | Women astronauts—United States—Biography—Juvenile
    literature. | Astronauts—United States—Biography—Juvenile literature.
Classification: LCC TL789.85.J46 L37 2017 (print) | LCC TL789.85.J46 (ebook) | DDC
    629.450092—dc23

LC record available at http://lccn.loc.gov/2015050918

Manufactured in the United States of America
1 – PC – 7/15/16

The images in this book are used with the permission of: © Jodi Jacobson/iStock.com, p. 4;
© AF archive/Alamy Stock Photo, pp. 5, 10; NASA, pp. 6, 9, 18, 21, 23; © Henryk Sadura/
Shutterstock.com, p. 8; © Science Picture Co/Science Source, p. 11; © turtix/Shutterstock.com,
p. 13; © Corbin O'Grady Studio/Science Source, p. 15; © Bettmann/Corbis, p. 17; Peace Corps
Media Library, p. 16; © Everett Historical/Shutterstock.com, p. 19; © Paramount/Courtesy:Everett
Collection, p. 24; © WENN Ltd/Alamy Stock Photo, p. 27.

Front Cover: © AP Images.

CONTENTS

CHAPTER 1
Pus and *Star Trek*   4

CHAPTER 2
Dancing, with Science   10

CHAPTER 3
Traveling to Space   18

CHAPTER 4
Bringing Science to Earth   24

Timeline   29
Source Notes   30
Glossary   30
Further Information   31
Index   32

Mae Jemison grew up in Chicago, Illinois.

PUS AND
STAR TREK

Mae Jemison loved everything about science, and it all started with pus. When she was a little girl in Chicago, she got a splinter in her thumb. It got infected. Pus oozed out of the wound. She thought it was one of the neatest things ever. Mae's mother told her to go look it up and learn more about it. Mae read about pus and got even more excited. She decided to become a scientist when she grew up.

Mae's parents believed that a good education was very important. They thought it was great that Mae liked science. They took her to the library and let her check out as many science books as she wanted.

STAR DREAMS FROM *STAR TREK*

When Mae was in elementary school, her favorite television show was *Star Trek*. One of the crew members on that show, Lieutenant Uhura, was a black woman. Lieutenant Uhura was

On *Star Trek*, Lieutenant Uhura (*second from right*) was communications officer for the starship *Enterprise*.

a talented scientist and officer. Mae imagined traveling to the stars just like Lieutenant Uhura.

At that time, there were very few women or black Americans in science. All the astronauts in the 1960s were white men. Seeing a black woman on a spaceship on television made Mae believe that black women could become astronauts. Because of *Star Trek*, Mae knew she was going to be in space one day.

The astronauts of the Apollo 11 mission prepare for a countdown demonstration test. This mission aimed to put humans on the surface of the moon.

TECH TALK

"As a little girl growing up on the south side of Chicago in the 1960s, I always knew I was going to be in space."

—*Mae Jemison*

ALWAYS ASKING QUESTIONS

In school, Mae loved asking and answering questions. One of Mae's teachers asked her what she wanted to be when she grew up. She said she wanted to be a scientist. Her teacher didn't think a black girl could be a scientist. She asked if Mae meant she wanted to be a nurse. Mae insisted that no, she meant a scientist.

Mae spent hours in her school library reading about science and astronomy. On the weekends, her parents took her to Chicago museums, including the Museum of Science and Industry. Mae wandered around the exhibits and learned that science was part of the whole world.

Mae loved high school. She got to study chemistry, biology, and physics. Mae made a good friend who shared her love of

Chicago's Museum of Science and Industry is one of the biggest science museums in the world.

Star Trek. They watched reruns of the show together every day after school. One day, while watching the show, Mae told her friend that she was going to be like Lieutenant Uhura when she grew up. Her friend thought Mae meant that she wanted to be a TV star. But what Mae really wanted was to go into space.

Mae and the rest of the world witnessed history on July 21, 1969, when astronauts Buzz Aldrin (*above*) and Neil Armstrong walked on the moon.

In high school, Mae performed in the All City High School production of *West Side Story*. Her favorite character was Anita, played in the movie by Rita Moreno (*center*).

DANCING,
WITH SCIENCE

There was only one thing Mae loved as much as science, and that was dance. Dancing made her feel as excited and free as science. She took lessons and became a very good dancer.

WORKING IN A REAL LABORATORY

When Mae was fifteen years old and a junior in high school, she did a science fair project. Mae wanted to learn about sickle cell anemia. Sickle cell anemia is a blood disease that commonly affects people of African ancestry.

Mae did not know how to start her project. But she knew that hospitals had laboratories that tested blood. She asked a local hospital if she could do research in their lab. The head of the lab agreed. He said that if she used his lab, she had to use it like a real scientist would. He made her do complex experiments and read scientific papers. It was the first time someone in science took Mae seriously. All the hard work paid off. She won first place at the science fair.

Sickle cell anemia causes red blood cells to take on a sickle shape.

Mae graduated from high school when she was only sixteen years old. She decided she wanted to be a **biomedical engineer**. Biomedical engineers invent machines and devices to use in medicine. This field combined Mae's love of science and her love of creativity. She was accepted at Stanford University in California, one of the best engineering schools.

CHALLENGES AND SETBACKS

College was a huge change for Jemison. She was the youngest engineering student at Stanford. She was a black woman. There were very few women or black people at Stanford when she arrived there in 1973.

Jemison was still an eager student. But one professor ignored her questions. When a white boy asked the same questions, the professor praised him. Jemison realized how hard it would be to be a black woman in the sciences.

Although Jemison had studied Russian in high school, one of her college professors did not believe she knew the language. He told her to take beginner Russian classes. It made Jemison feel like she did not know anything. She never took Russian classes at Stanford, even though she had chosen to study the language in high school because she thought it would be important in science and space exploration.

Jemison encountered discrimination while studying engineering at Stanford University.

DANCER OR DOCTOR?

Fortunately, Jemison's other professors supported and respected her. She did not let the sexism and racism she experienced in college stop her. Jemison was determined to pursue her goal of becoming a biomedical engineer. Since biomedical engineering was a new area of study at that time, Jemison graduated with a degree in **chemical engineering** instead.

Jemison was not sure what to do next. She thought about medical school. If she was going to be a biomedical engineer, it would help her to know about medicine too.

But Jemison also still loved dancing. She thought about becoming a professional dancer. Her mother told her she could still dance if she was a doctor, but she couldn't doctor if she was a dancer. That made up Jemison's mind. She moved to

EMI SCANNER

Electrical engineer Godfrey Hounsfield invented the CT scanner, an important biomedical breakthrough of the 1970s. The device lets doctors look inside a patient's body without surgery.

New York City to attend Cornell University's medical school. She worked hard and graduated with a medical degree.

A DOCTOR WITH SPACE DREAMS

Jemison never planned to practice medicine. She still wanted to be a biomedical engineer. Her plan was to go back to engineering school after medical school.

But she also wanted to travel and see the world. She joined the Peace Corps as a doctor in West Africa, where she served

In January 1980, a group of Peace Corps volunteers attend a seminar on public health nursing at the Serabu Hospital in Sierra Leone.

as the medical officer for corps members in Sierra Leone and Liberia. While there, she also taught and did medical research. The hospitals Jemison worked in did not have modern equipment. This experience made her realize how much she wanted to help people through technology.

After two and a half years with the Peace Corps, Jemison came back to the United States. She went to work as a doctor in Los Angeles. She kept taking engineering classes. But Jemison still dreamed of space. In 1985, she decided to apply to the National Aeronautics and Space Administration (NASA) to become an astronaut.

Jemison works at the desk of her medical office in Los Angeles.

Chapter 3

NASA's space shuttle *Atlantis* completed a successful seven-day mission in December 1985.

TRAVELING TO SPACE

In 1985, NASA's space shuttle program was going strong. The world marveled at the astronauts who went into space. Jemison realized this was her chance to become an astronaut. She sent in an application.

Then, on January 28, 1986, the space shuttle *Challenger* exploded on liftoff. The disaster was shown on live television. The world was stunned. NASA shut down the shuttle program until its engineers could find out what had gone wrong.

Like everyone else, Jemison wondered if the shuttles would ever go into space again. But in the fall of 1986, NASA announced it was looking for astronauts. Jemison sent in a new application. Then she waited.

Plumes of gas formed after the explosion of the space shuttle *Challenger*.

NASA CALLING

A few weeks later, NASA called to invite Jemison to the Johnson Space Center in Houston, Texas, for interviews! More than two thousand people had applied, but only one hundred were interviewed. Of those, fifteen people would be chosen for the astronaut program.

For a week, doctors examined Jemison. They did X-rays and blood tests. They measured her strength. They asked her questions about her life and her work. Then she went home to wait some more.

One day, the phone rang in her clinic. A man from NASA was calling to tell her that she had been chosen to be an astronaut. But she could not tell anyone until NASA made the official announcement the next day. Jemison went home, bursting with the news. But she had to wait to tell anyone! So she celebrated by watching reruns of *Star Trek*.

TRAINING FOR SPACE

Jemison moved to Houston to start astronaut training. The first part of training took two years. Jemison and her fellow astronauts learned about space flight. They took classes in Earth sciences, **meteorology**, space science, and engineering.

They also took lessons on survival training, scuba diving, and how to fly an airplane.

After this training, each astronaut was given his or her mission assignment. Jemison was going into space as a mission specialist. In this role she would conduct scientific experiments on the mission. For three more years, Jemison trained with experienced astronauts. She learned how to work in weightless conditions. She also learned how to do the experiments she would be working on during the space flight.

EIGHT DAYS IN ORBIT

Finally, on September 12, 1992, Jemison took off on the space shuttle *Endeavour* as the first black woman in space. The first thing Jemison saw from space was her hometown of Chicago. As she gazed at the city, 191 miles (307 kilometers) below, she

Jemison (*top row, second from right*) and her fellow crew members trained for their flight into space.

TECH TALK

"It is important . . . for young black girls to see me aboard exploring space. But it is just as critical that older white men who make so many decisions about engineering scholarships see me and understand the talent and potential of those girls."

—Mae Jemison

smiled. She thought of that little girl who dreamed of being an astronaut so long ago. She had made it to space!

But there was work to do. Jemison was in charge of experiments to test how space affects human bone cells. She also worked on experiments that measured the effects of space motion sickness.

Every astronaut got to take a few special items into space with them. Jemison brought a poster of the Alvin Ailey American Dance Company. But she could not forget Lieutenant Uhura. So each morning, she started her shift by calling to NASA with one of Uhura's famous lines from the show.

For eight days, she and her fellow astronauts orbited Earth and conducted more than forty experiments. Then it was time to come home.

On *Endeavour*, Jemison conducted scientific experiments on space motion sickness and the effects of weightlessness on bone cells.

Chapter 4

Jemison (*left*) appears on the set of *Star Trek: The Next Generation.*

BRINGING SCIENCE TO EARTH

Jemison's dream of space flight had come true. But now she had to decide what to do next. She thought about staying in the space program. She also thought about her ambition to use science to help the world. She decided to leave

NASA and figure out ways to use technology to help others. But first, Jemison would have another exciting opportunity.

Soon after Jemison returned from space, she got an amazing phone call. The makers of the television series *Star Trek: The Next Generation* wanted her to appear on the show! Of course, she jumped at the chance. Jemison was the first real astronaut to appear on the show.

SCIENCE AND TECHNOLOGY FOR EVERYONE

That same year, Jemison created a company called the Jemison Group. The Jemison Group designs and creates technologies that help people around the world. It has helped design solar energy **generators** and **satellite** communications systems for poor areas in developing countries.

TECH TALK

"Space isn't just for rocket scientists and billionaires; it's a part of all of us."

—Mae Jemison

Jemison also started the Dorothy Jemison Foundation for Excellence. It is named after her mother, who was a teacher. The foundation helps teachers teach science and technology to kids. Jemison also started a science camp where kids from around the world can learn how to use science and technology to help Earth.

But Jemison wanted to find even more ways to teach. She decided to become a college professor. She taught at Dartmouth College, where she also started the Jemison Institute. The institute works to establish new technologies that can be used in developing countries.

After a few years, Jemison decided she was ready for another new challenge. She quit her job so she could speak to students and adults around the world about science and technology.

LOOKING TO THE FUTURE OF SPACE TRAVEL

Today, Jemison works with NASA again. But this time she is not an astronaut. She is one of the leaders of the 100 Year Starship project. The project focuses on inventing systems that humans would need for **interstellar** travel in one hundred years.

Jemison speaks to an audience of high school students at a Women's History Month celebration in 2009.

The project asks questions such as, How do you make air on a ship in space for many years? How would you make a steady supply of food and water? Where would the power for the ship come from? These systems will have to be ready before anyone can start to build a ship that will go to the stars. Another part of the 100 Year Starship project is finding ways this space technology will help people on Earth.

In the 100 Year Starship project, Jemison found the perfect job. It combines science and creativity to make technologies that can help people live on Earth and explore space. Jemison might be on Earth for good, but she is still following her star dreams.

TECH TALK

"Science is very important to me, but I also like to stress that you have to be well-rounded. One's love for science doesn't get rid of all the other areas. I truly feel someone interested in science is interested in understanding what's going on in the world."

—*Mae Jemison*

TIMELINE

1956

Mae Jemison is born on October 17.

1977

Jemison graduates from Stanford University with a degree in chemical engineering.

1981

Jemison graduates from Cornell University with a degree in medicine.

1983

Jemison joins the Peace Corps as a medical officer.

1986

The space shuttle *Challenger* explodes after liftoff on January 28.

1987

Jemison becomes the first black woman to be accepted into the space program.

1992

On September 12, *Endeavour* blasts into space with Mission Specialist Jemison on board.

1993

Jemison resigns from NASA and creates the Jemison Group.

1995

Jemison becomes Professor of Environmental Studies at Dartmouth College.

2012

Jemison becomes head of the 100 Year Starship project.

SOURCE NOTES

7 Camille Jackson, "The Legacy of Lt. Uhura: Astronaut Mae Jemison on Race in Space," *Duke Today*, October 28, 2013, https://today.duke.edu/2013/10/maejemison.

12 Dr. Mae Jemison, *Find Where the Wind Goes* (New York: Scholastic, 2002), 78.

14 Ibid., 124.

22 Dr. Mae Jemison, "The Space Age, Race and a Quiet Revolution," *The Huffington Post*, February 28, 2014, http://www.huffingtonpost.com/dr-mae-jemison/the-space-age-race-and-a-quiet-revolution_b_4875029.html.

25 Mae Jemison, "All Aboard the 100 Year Starship," *Scientific American*, June 11, 2014, http://blogs.scientificamerican.com/guest-blog/all-aboard-the-100-year-starship.

28 Marcia C. Johnson, "Upward with Worldly Lessons," *Greensboro News and Record* (January 28, 1991): B5.

GLOSSARY

biomedical engineering
  a type of engineering that deals with the design of medical devices

chemical engineering
  a type of engineering that deals with the use of chemistry in industry

generator
  a machine that converts one kind of energy to another

interstellar
  space beyond our solar system

meteorology
  the science of weather

satellite
  an object that orbits a planet

FURTHER INFORMATION

BOOKS

Jemison, Mae, and Dana Meachen Rau. *The 100 Year Starship.* New York: Scholastic, 2013. Learn more about the 100 Year Starship project from Jemison herself.

Kruesi, Liz. *Discover Space Exploration.* Minneapolis: Lerner Publications, 2017. Find out about the science of space exploration.

Woods, Mary B. and Michael Woods. *Space Disasters.* Minneapolis: Lerner Publications, 2008. Learn more about the *Challenger* explosion and other space disasters.

WEBSITES

100 Year Starship
http://100yss.org
Learn about the 100 Year Starship project.

The Secret Life of Scientists and Engineers: Mae Jemison
**http://www.pbs.org/wgbh/nova/blogs/secretlife/space
-science/mae-jemison**
Watch interviews with Mae Jemison about dance, space, and her appearance on *Star Trek: The Next Generation*.

Teach Arts and Sciences Together
**https://www.ted.com/talks/mae_jemison_on_teaching_arts_and
_sciences_together**
Watch Mae Jemison's 2002 TED Talk about the relationship between science and the arts.

LERNER

SOURCE

Expand learning beyond the printed book. Download free, complementary educational resources for this book from our website, www.lernersource.com.

INDEX

100 Year Starship project, 26, 28

Alvin Ailey American Dance Company, 22

Challenger, 19

Chicago, Illinois, 4, 8, 21

Cornell University, 15

dance, 10, 14, 22

Dartmouth College, 26

Dorothy Jemison Foundation, 26

Endeavour, 21

engineering, 12, 14–16, 20, 22

Houston, Texas, 20

Jemison Group, 25

Jemison Institute, 26

Johnson Space Center, 20

Liberia, 16

Los Angeles, California, 16

meteorology, 20

Museum of Science and Industry, 7

National Aeronautics and Space Administration (NASA), 16, 18–20, 22, 23–24, 26

New York City, 14–15

Peace Corps, 15–16

pus, 4–5

racism, 14

satellite communications systems, 25

sexism, 14

sickle cell anemia, 11, 12

Sierra Leone, 16

solar energy generators, 25

space shuttles, 18–19, 21

Stanford University, 12–13

Star Trek, 5–6, 8, 20

Star Trek: The Next Generation, 25

Uhura, Lieutenant, 5–6, 8, 22

ABOUT THE AUTHOR

Allison Lassieur still remembers the first time she watched *Star Trek* on television as a child, and she's been a proud nerd ever since. She has written more than 150 books for kids about history, science, current events, and strange unsolved mysteries. Allison lives in a house in the Tennessee woods with her husband, daughter, three dogs, two cats, and too many books.